LAUGH AND LEARN

KIDS' JOKES

Over 300 Hilarious Jokes and Fascinating Facts

John Decherd

ISBN-13:   978-1523268344

ISBN-10:   1523268344

Printed in the United States of America

I dedicate this book to my young sons - Micah, Jonathan, and Elijah- who are beginning to find joy in hearing and telling jokes. I also dedicate this to my father-in-law, Ray Tolar, who always enjoys telling a good joke to others.

CONTENTS

PART ONE

Q & A JOKES

Q: What is a cheetah's favorite thing to eat?
A: Fast food!

Fact: Cheetahs can run up to 70 miles per hour and can go this fast in just 3 seconds! There are less than 10,000 cheetahs left in the wild making them Africa's most endangered large cat.

Q: What do you call a cow in a tornado?
A: A milkshake!

Fact: Extreme tornadoes can reach wind speeds of over 300 miles per hour. Small tornadoes sometimes form on the edge of bigger tornadoes.

Q: What happened when the monster ate the electric company?
A: He was in shock for a week.

Fact: Electricity travels at the speed of light -- more than 186,000 miles per second!

Q: What musical instrument is found in the bathroom?
A: A tuba toothpaste

Fact: Before toothpaste was invented, people used dry, rough objects to clean their teeth such as pumice (volcano rock) and crushed egg shell! They also used twigs and their fingers to brush!

Q: What do you call cheese that's not yours?
A: Nacho cheese!

Fact: The most popular cheese recipe is the United States is "macaroni and cheese." There are over 2,000 varieties of cheeses.

Q: Where do pencils go for vacation?
A: Pencil-vania.

Fact: It's said that the average pencil can draw a line 35 miles long before it is used up. Pencils can also write in zero gravity on space missions.

Q: Why did the girl smear peanut butter on the road?
A: To go with the traffic jam!

Fact: It takes about 540 peanuts to make one 12-ounce jar of peanut butter.

Q: Which flower talks the most?
A: Tulips, of course, because they have *two* lips!

Fact: Tulips used to be the most expensive flower in the world. In fact, at one point in history, tulips were even more expensive than people's homes.

Q: How do you cut a wave in half?
A: Use a sea saw.

Fact: Many things can cause waves in water, but the most common cause is wind blowing across the surface.

Q: Why do bananas have to put on sunscreen before they go to the beach?
A: Because they might peel!

Fact: Bananas contain around 75% water. They are a high nutritional food and a healthy snack.

Q: How do you make a tissue dance?
A: You put a little boogie in it.

Fact: The speed of a sneeze is about 100 mph. That's faster than a cheetah can run. A sneeze can also spread 100,000 germs in the air.

Q: Which dinosaur knew the most words?
A: The thesaurus.

Fact: No one knows exactly how long dinosaurs could live, but some scientists think some dinosaurs could live over 200 years.

Q: What did the mushroom say to the fungus?
A: You're a fun guy.

Fact: Mushrooms are fungi. Fungi recycle plants after they die. Without fungi the earth would be covered in several feet of dead plants and all plant life would die.

Q: Why did the cat go to Minnesota?
A: To get a mini soda!

Fact: Cats are the most popular pet in the United States. There are 88 million cats and 74 million dogs.

Q: Who did Frankenstein the monster bring to prom?
A: His ghoulfriend.

Fact: Frankenstein is not real, but the story came about as a competition between Mary Shelly, her husband, and another man as to who could write the best horror story.

Q: Where do orcas hear music?
A: Orca-stras!

Fact: Orcas are also called killer whales and belong to the dolphin family. They don't normally attack humans.

Q: What do you do if your dog chews a dictionary?
A: Take the words out of his mouth!

Fact: Approximately one new word is added to the English language every two hours, and 4,000 new words are added to the English dictionary each year.

Q: What do you call lending money to a bison?
A: A buff-a-loan.

Fact: Bison are North America's largest land animal. A bison stands over 6 feet tall and 10 feet long.

Q: What is black, white, and red all over?
A: A sunburnt penguin!

Fact: Penguins don't have wings, they have flippers. A cold and icy as it is, no penguins live at the North Pole.

Q: What do bees chew?
A: Bumble gum!

Fact: Honey bees from a typical hive visit approximately 225,000 flowers per day. Bees must visit approximately 2 million flowers and fly over 55,000 miles to make 1 pound of honey.

A team of little animals and a team of big animals decided to play football. During the first half of the game, the big animals were winning. But during the second half, a centipede scored so many touchdowns that the little animals won the game. When the game was over, the chipmunk asked the centipede, "Where were you during the first half?" He replied "Putting on my shoes!"

Fact: All centipedes are predators (eat other creatures). The first segment of their legs are not for walking, they are venomous fangs they inject their prey with poison.

Q: What is as big as an elephant but weighs nothing?
A: Its shadow!

Fact: Although they are the worlds larges land mammal, Elephants can swim. They use their trunk to breathe like a snorkel in deep water.

Q: Where does an elephant pack his luggage?
A: In his trunk!

Fact: The elephant's trunk is able to sense the size, shape and temperature of an object. An elephant uses its trunk to lift food and suck up water then pour it into its mouth.

Q: What do you call an exploding monkey?
A: A baboom!

Fact: Most monkeys eat both plants and animals, and some monkeys also eat dirt. Monkeys have tails, apes do not.

Q: What fish only swims at night?
A: A starfish.

Fact: Starfish are also called sea stars and they are not fish. If a starfish loses an arm it can grow another one.

Q: What was the first animal in space?
A: The cow that jumped over the moon!

Fact: Cows drink almost as much as a bathtub full of water each day. They can live more than 20 years.

Q: Where do fish keep their money?
A: In a river bank!

Fact: A bank is an organization where you can place your money for safekeeping. When you use a debit card or write a check money is taken from your bank account to pay it.

Q: What do you call a dinosaur in a car accident?
A: A tyrannosaurus wreck!

Fact: The largest tooth of any carnivorous (meat eating) dinosaur is that of a Tyrannosaurus Rex and is one foot long.

Q: Why are giraffes so slow to apologize?
A: It takes them a long time to swallow their pride.

Fact: The giraffe is the tallest land animal in the world standing between 16-18 feet tall. They only sleep about 2 hours a day.

Q: Why was the mouse afraid of the water?
A: Catfish

Fact: The entire body of the catfish is covered with taste buds that can detect chemicals in the water and respond to touch. A catfish can live 8-20 years in the wild.

Q: What is King Arthur's favorite fish?
A: A swordfish.

Fact: Swordfish are one of the fastest fish in the ocean and can swim over 50 miles an hour.

Q: What is a shark's favorite sandwich?
A: Peanut butter and jellyfish.

Fact: Sharks have to be constantly moving to force water over their gills so they can breathe. If they didn't, they would suffocate and die.

Q: How many skunks does it take to make a big stink?
A: A phew.

Fact: Skunks are nocturnal, meaning they are most active at night. They can spray their stinky mist up to 10 feet away and you can smell it up to 1.5 miles away.

Q: Where are sharks from?
A: Finland.

Fact: Sharks do not have a single bone in their body. Instead they have a skeleton made up of cartilage; the same flexible tissue that makes up the inside of your nose and ears.

Q: What does an octopus wear when it gets cold?
A: A coat of arms.

Fact: Octopuses are one of the smartest invertebrates (no back bone). They learn easily and can solve problems. An octopus has three hearts. Two pump blood through the gills, and another pumps blood through their body.

Q: Why don't bears wear shoes?
A: What's the use, they'd still have bear feet!

Fact: Bears care deeply about family members. They will risk their lives and even fight to the death in order to save a cub or sibling from danger.

Q: What's worse than a centipede with athlete's foot?

A: A porcupine with split ends!

Fact: A porcupine has approximately 30,000 needle sharp quills on its body. But a porcupine cannot shoot or throw its quills as some people think.

Q: What's a frog's favorite drink?
A: Croak-a-cola.

Fact: Frogs don't need to drink water. They absorb it through their skin. The croak of some frogs can be heard up to a mile away.

Q: What do you call snake with no clothes on?
A: Snaked.

Fact: There is only one continent in the world in which there are no snakes — Antarctica. Snakes smell with their tongue.

Q: What's an alligator's favorite drink?
A: Gator-Ade.

Fact: Alligators don't just eat meat. They will eat fruit also, when they can get it. Large alligators can bite with 2,900 pounds of force. That's like having the weight of a car sitting on top of you.

Q: What do you call a dinosaur at the rodeo?
A: A Broncosaurus or a Tyrannosaurus Tex.

Fact: The Brontosaurus is one of the largest animals to have ever walked the earth. It could grow up to 75 feet long and weigh 25 tons.

Q: What do camels use to hide themselves?
A: Camelflauge!

Fact: Camels do not store water in their humps. The humps are for storing fatty tissue which provides them energy when they need it.

Q: What do you call a cow that twitches?
A: Beef jerky.

Fact: Beef Jerky is astronaut food! NASA has been providing space shuttle crews this lightweight high protein treat since the mid-nineties. However, beef jerky has a lot of salt so don't eat too much.

Q: How do chickens get strong?
A: Egg-cersize.

Fact: The chicken is the closest living relative to the great Tyrannosaurus-Rex, believe it or not!

Q: Why do pandas like old movies?
A: Because they are black and white.

Fact: A panda is more similar to a raccoon that a bear. The giant panda feeds almost exclusively on the stems, leaves and fresh young shoots of the bamboo plant.

Q: What did the porcupine say to the cactus?
A: Is that you mommy?

Fact: The spines (thorns) on a cactus are really a type of leaf. They help protect the cactus from animals that might try to get the water and liquid inside.

Q: What kind of math do Snowy Owls like?
A: Owlgebra.

Fact: Barn Owls swallow their prey whole—skin, bones, and all—and they eat up to 1,000 mice each year.

Q: Why does a stork stand on one leg?
A: Because it would fall over if it lifted the other one.

Fact: Storks make huge nests in trees, on cliffs, on roofs or even on the tops of telephone poles. The nests are used year after year. They can be 9 feet wide or larger.

Q: Why do hummingbirds hum?
A: Because they don't know the words.

Fact: Some hummingbirds are so small, they have been known to be caught by dragonflies and praying mantis, trapped in spider's webs, snatched by frogs and stuck on thistles.

There was a duck who walked into a store and said, "Got any candy?" The storekeeper said, "No, we don't." The next day, the duck went into the same store and asked the same thing and got the same answer. The duck kept going back every day for a week and asked the same thing and kept getting the same answer until the store keeper got so angry he said, "If you come in here and ask that again, I will hit you on the head with a hammer!" The next day, the duck walks into the store and asks, "Got a hammer?" The store keeper says, "No." Then the duck asks, "Got any candy?"

Fact: Ducks are omnivorous (eat everything) eaters and will eat grass, aquatic plants, insects, seeds, fruit, fish, crustaceans and other types of food.

A man had a pet centipede. He said, "centipede, go get the paper and make it snappy!"
A half an hour later the man went outside and said, "I thought I told you to get the paper a half an hour ago!"
"Well, I had to put on my shoes," said the centipede.

Fact: Centipedes don't always have exactly 100 legs. The can have a lot more or a lot less.

Q: Why did the fly never land on the computer?
A: He was afraid of the World Wide Web.

Fact: House flies taste with their feet, which are much more sensitive to the taste of sugar than your tongue.

A man was looking out his window when he noticed that there was a snail on one of his plants. So he took the snail and threw him as far as he could. Ten years later the old man heard a tap, tap, tap on his window, and when he looked up he saw a very cross snail who looked at him and
said, "Hey, what did you do that for?"

Fact: Snails may be very small, but they are also very strong. They can lift 10 times their own body weight.

Q: What's worse than a worm in your apple?
A: Half a worm.

Fact: Apples are actually part of the rose family like pears and plums. Apple trees can live more than 100 years.

Q: What do you call two ants that run away to get married?
A: Ant-elopes!

Fact: Ants can carry objects 50 times their own body weight. Ants were around when dinosaurs lived.

Q: Why didn't the skeleton cross the road?
A: He didn't have any guts!

Fact: You have more bones when you are born than you do as an adult. When you are born you have around 300 bones, but as an adult many bones have fused and you have 206.

Q: What does a cat call a hummingbird?
A: Fast food.

Fact: Hummingbirds can fly backwards, and are the only group of birds able to do so.

Q: Why didn't the skeleton go to the ball?
A: Because he had no BODY to go with.

Fact: Your largest bone is in your thigh (upper leg) and is called the femur. Your smallest bone is in your ear and is called the stirrup.

Q: What is a vampire's favorite fruit?
A: A neck-tarine!

Fact: A rare disease called *porphyria* causes vampire-like symptoms, such as an extreme sensitivity to sunlight and sometimes hairiness. In extreme cases, teeth might be stained reddish brown, and eventually the person may go mad.

Q: What kind of dessert does a ghost like?
A: I scream!

Fact: Before ice cream was made with milk, it was indeed made with ice.

Q: What do you get when you cross a snowman with a vampire?

A: Frostbite.

Fact: Frostbite is when your skin and body tissue freezes. It can be very dangerous and painful. Kids are more likely to be frost bitten than adults.

Q: What kind of pants do ghosts wear?
A: Boo-Jeans.

Fact: Blue jeans are actually indigo color. They were originally given this color because it helps to hide stains and dirt better than lighter colors.

Q: What did one owl say to the other owl?
A: Happy Owl-ween!

Fact: Owls can see things far away very well, but they can't see things closely very well.

Q. What did one volcano say to the other?
A: I lava you.

Fact: Hot liquid rock under the earth is called magma. When it comes out of the earth it is called lava.

Q: What did the octopus say to his girlfriend when he proposed?

A: Can I have your hand, hand, hand, hand, hand, hand, hand, hand in marriage?

Fact: Octopuses can lose an arm to a predator to escape and regrow it later.

Q: Where was the Declaration of Independence signed?
A: On the bottom.

Fact: The signers of the Declaration of Independence did not all sign on the same day.

Q: What do you get when you cross a cow with a trampoline?
A: A milkshake!

Fact: Milkshakes used to be considered a health food. This isn't true anymore.

Q: What do you get when you cross a karate expert with a pig?
A: A pork chop.

Fact: Elvis Presley was a black belt in karate. Karate originally began in India then developed later in China.

Q: What do you get when you cross a fish and drumsticks?
A: Fishsticks.

Fact: Drums are considered one of the world's oldest musical instruments.

Q: What do you get when you cross a tiger and a blizzard?
A: Frostbite!

Fact: A blizzard is a severe snowstorm that usually has very cold temperatures and high winds.

Q: What do you get when you cross a caterpillar and a parrot?
A: A walkie talkie!

Fact: Parrots are thought to be one of the most intelligent bird species and some parrots can live over 80 years.

Q: What do you get when you cross a fish with an elephant?
A: Swimming trunks.

Fact: Elephants can swim as much as 20 miles a day using their trunk as a natural snorkel.

Q: What do you get when you cross a lemon and a cat?
A: A sourpuss.

Fact: Lemon juice on your skin can be an effective insect repellant.

Q: What do you get when you cross a hamburger with a computer?
A: A big mac!

Fact: 50 billion burgers are eaten in the United States each year!

Q: What do you get if you cross a kangaroo and a snake?
A: A jump rope!

Fact: Jumping rope is good for your heart, helps relax you, and is excellent exercise.

Q: What do you call a cat crossed with a fish?
A: Catfish.

Fact: One catfish can lay 4000 eggs per pound of body weight per year. So a 4 pound catfish can lay 16,000 eggs per year!

Q: What do you get when you cross a porcupine and a turtle?
A: A slowpoke.

Fact: The word "porcupine" means thorny pig.

Q: What do you call a dog on the beach in the Summer?
A: A hot dog!

Fact: Hot dogs were first made in Germany, and in the United States most people like mustard as their favorite topping.

Q. How you mend a broken pumpkin?
A: With a pumpkin patch!

Fact: Pumpkins are fruits and are over 90 percent water. Each pumpkins has over 500 seeds.

Q: How do Eskimos make their beds?
A: With sheets of ice and blankets of snow.

Fact: Eskimos prefer to be called Inuit or Inuk.

Q: Why don't mountains get cold in the winter?
A: They wear snowcaps.

Fact: The tallest known mountain in the solar system is Olympus Mons, located on Mars.

Q: What do you call a snowman in the desert?
A: A puddle!

Fact: Around one third of the Earth's surface is covered in deserts.

Q: What is a snowman's favorite breakfast?
A: Frosted Flakes!

Fact: Americans consume 101 pounds or 160 bowls of cereal per person every year.

Q: What's the slipperiest country?
A: Greece!

Fact: The Olympic Games originated in Ancient Greece.

Q: Why can't you say a joke while standing on ice?
A: Because it might crack up!

Fact: Before the refrigerator, people used to harvest ice and sell it. The large ice chunks would be placed in a home's "ice box" to keep food cold.

Q: Why did the orange stop in the middle of the hill?
A: It ran out of juice!

Fact: Around 85% of oranges are used to produce orange juice.

Q: Why are the floors of basketball courts always so damp?
A: The players dribble a lot.

Fact: Until 1929 basketball was actually played with soccer balls.

Q: Why is tennis such a loud game?
A: Because each player raises a racquet.

Fact: The longest tennis match ever lasted 11 hours!

Q: What do you call a boomerang that won't come back?
A: A stick.

Fact: Most boomerangs don't come back and were never intended to do so. Those that do return are usually used for fun.

Q: Why was the math book sad?
A: It had too many problems.

Fact: More people say their most popular favorite number is 7.

Q: Why did the belt go to jail?
A: It held up a pair of pants.

Fact: There are over 5,000 prisons and jails in the United States.

Q: What did the light bulb say to its mother?
A: I wuv you watts and watts.

Fact: Early light bulbs tended to explode, so they weren't used much until the 1920s.

Q: What's the tallest building in the world?
A: The library, because it has the most stories.

Fact: Actually the tallest building in the world is the Burj Khalifa in Dubai, United Arab Emirates and is over 2,700 feet tall.

Q: What kind of phones do people in jail use?
A: Cell phones.

Fact: The fear of having no cell phone signal or being unable to make or receive cell phone calls is called Nomophobia.

Q: What do you call a king who is only 12 inches tall?
A: A ruler.

Fact: A ruler is a straightened strip of wood, metal or plastic used for drawing straight lines or measuring lengths.

Q: Why did the computer squeak?
A: Someone stepped on its mouse.

Fact: The computer mouse is named a "mouse" because it's kind of shaped like the rodent it's named after — the mouse

Q: Which runs faster, hot or cold water?
A: Hot, because you can catch cold.

Fact: About 70-80% of your body is made up of water. So you need to be sure to drink enough of it each day.

Q: How does the ocean say hello?
A: It waves.

Fact: The largest ocean on earth is the Pacific Ocean, covering 30% of the earth.

Q: Why did the boy take a ladder to school?
A: He wanted to go to high school!

Fact: More than 90,000 people have to go to the emergency room each year due to ladder injuries. So be careful!

Q: Why would Snow White make a great judge?
A: She was the fairest in the land.

Fact: Walt Disney came up with the idea of Snow White and the Seven Dwarves when he was 15 years old.

Q: What kind of underwear do reporters wear?
A: News briefs.

Fact: The average American owns approximately 21 pairs of underwear!

Q: What bee is good for your health?
A: Vitamin bee!

Fact: Honey is the only food that includes all the substances necessary to sustain life, including enzymes, vitamins, minerals, and water.

Q: Why did the strawberry call 911?
A: It was in a jam!

Fact: Strawberries are the only fruit that wear their seeds on the outside.

Q: Why was the baseball game so hot?
A: Because all the fans left!

Fact: The New York Yankees have won 26 World Series titles, more than any other Major League baseball team.

Q: What do you call a story about a broken pencil?
A: Pointless.

Fact: Before erasers were invented, writers used breadcrumbs to erase their pencil mistakes.

Q: What do you give a lemon in distress?
A: Lemonade.

Fact: Lemonade has been around a long time. It is first mentioned in ancient Egyptian writings.

Q: What's a tree's favorite drink?
A: Root beer.

Fact: Root beer is made out of 16 different roots and herbs. Sassafras is one of these.

Q: What do you call a fairy who doesn't take a bath?
A: Stinker Bell.

Fact: In the movie *Peter Pan,* Tinker Bell, the fairy, enjoys a diet of candy, tea, and pumpkin muffins.

Q: What do you call two banana peels?
A: Slippers.

Fact: Bananas are picked unripe green and then ripened in special storage chambers using ethylene.

Q: Why did the melon jump into the lake?
A: It wanted to be a watermelon.

Fact: A watermelon contains about 6% sugar and 92% water. It is considered both a fruit and a vegetable.

Q: What has four wheels and flies?
A: A garbage truck.

Fact: The average American throws away more than 7 pounds of garbage a day. That's 102 tons in a lifetime, more than any other country.

Q: Why can't a bicycle stand up?
A: Because it's two tired!

Fact: The bicycle is the most efficient vehicle ever devised; a human on a bicycle is more efficient than a train, truck, airplane, boat, car, motorcycle or jet pack.

Q: What did the belly button say just before it left?
A: I'm outtie here!

Fact: Innie belly buttons are more common than outtie belly buttons. Having an innie or an outtie depends on how the doctor ties the umbilical cord.

Q: What do a baker and a millionaire have in common?
A: They are both rolling in the dough!

Fact: Millionaires often start saving earlier than most people and spend wiser.

Q: What did the teddy bear say when it was offered dessert?
A: No thank you, I'm stuffed.

Fact: Bear toys used to be called "Bruins" until they became stuffed and then were called "Teddy Bears."

A man was looking for a person to paint his porch, so he hired a young lady and told her what to do. After about 30 minutes, the lady came to the door and said "I'm done." The man asked "how did you get done so fast?" The lady said "it was hard at first, but it got easier towards the end. And by the way, it's a Ferrari not a Porsche."

Fact: The Greek philosopher Plato is credited with the discovery that you can mix two different paint colors together to produce a third color.

Q: Why did the sea monster eat five ships that were carrying potatoes?
A: No one can eat just one potato ship.

Fact: Thomas Jefferson gets the credit for introducing "French fries" to America when he served them at a White House dinner.

Q: How did Ben Franklin feel after discovering electricity?
A: Shocked.

Fact: Birds can sit safely on a power line without getting shocked because they are just touching one line. If they touched two lines with a wing or foot they would create a circuit and would be electrocuted.

Q: Why did the football coach go to the bank?
A: To get his quarterback.

Fact: During a regular NFL game you are likely to watch the following: 11 minutes of actual playing time, 3 seconds of cheerleaders, 17 minutes of replays and 67 minutes of players just standing there

Q: What washes up on small beaches?
A: Microwaves.

Fact: Microwaving food can decrease its nutritional food value.

Q: What is only a small box but can weigh over a hundred pounds?
A: A scale.

Fact: People who weigh themselves more frequently are more likely to lose weight than those who don't.

Q: What has holes all over and holds water?
A: A sponge!

Fact: Some deep-water sponges can live to be over 200 years old.

Q: What do lawyers wear in court?
A: Lawsuits.

Fact: A lawsuit is a dispute between people or organizations that is brought to court to be decided.

Q: Why don't honest people need beds?
A: They don't lie.

Fact: Honest Tea's study of honesty found that women (95%) are a bit more honest than men (91%).

Q: How can five people be under the same small umbrella and not get wet?
A: It wasn't raining!

Fact: Modern day umbrellas are coated with Teflon, which makes their canopy waterproof.

Q: What's 182 feet tall and made out of pepperoni and cheese?
A: The leaning tower of Pizza.

Fact: The Leaning Tower of Pisa leans because of the heavy weight of the building and the soft soil it was built on.

Q: How are doughnuts and golf alike?
A: They both have a hole in one!

Fact: Doughnuts used to be called "olykoeks" which means "oily cakes" in Dutch.

Q: What is a baby bee?
A: A little humbug!

Fact: Queen Bees will lay as many as 2000 eggs on a good day and an average of one every 45 seconds.

Q: Why did the Oreo go to the dentist?
A: To get his filling!

Fact: Oreo cookies are the world's bestselling cookie having sold over 450 billion since 1912.

Q: Why did a boy throw a clock out the window?
A: To see time fly.

Fact: Times always moves forward and never backwards.

Q: What are pirate's favorite treat?
A: Chips AHOY!!

Fact: The official state cookie of both Massachusetts and Pennsylvania is the chocolate chip cookie.

Q: What did the baby corn ask the mother corn?
A: Where is popcorn?

Fact: Popcorn kernels can pop up to three feet in the air.

Q: Where do cars go for a swim?
A: At the carpool!

Fact: Carpooling is when several people decide to share the same car when they are going somewhere. This saves a lot of energy and money.

Q: Why did the boy put candy under his pillow?
A: Because he wanted sweet dreams.

Fact: Dreaming can help you learn and solve problems. When you dream your brain is often actively thinking and solving problems you encounter when you are awake.

Q: Why did the spy stay in bed?
A: Because he was under cover.

Fact: Spies seek out secret information and pass it on to others. Being a spy can be dangerous work.

Q: Why did the tomato blush?
A: Because he saw the salad dressing!

Fact: The biggest tomato fight in the world happens each year in the small Spanish town of Buñol. The festival called La Tomatina, involves some 40,000 people throwing 150,000 tomatoes at each other.

Q: What's a royal pardon?
A: It's what the queen says after she burps.

Fact: Actually, a royal pardon is an official order given by a king or queen to stop the punishment of a person accused of a crime.

A rope walked into a restaurant and ordered a milkshake. The waiter said "Are you a rope?" The rope said "Yes." The waiter said "We don't serve ropes." So, the rope went out and burnt off his ends and tied himself into a knot. The rope went back into the restaurant and ordered a milkshake. The waiter asked "Are you a rope?" The rope said "No, I'm a-frayed knot."

Fact: Anytime you tie a knot in a rope, you weaken it; in drop tests and pull tests, a rope typically breaks at the knot.

Q: How do Vikings send secret messages?
A: Norse code.

Fact: Vikings loved their boats. Often distinguished raiders and prominent women were buried in ships, surrounded by weapons, valuable goods and sometimes even sacrificed slaves.

Q: Why should you never tell a secret in a corn field?
A: Because there are too many ears.

Fact: Corn is called maize in most countries.

Q: Why did the TV cross the road?
A: Because it wanted to be a flat screen.

Fact: Televisions first went on sale in the late 1920's and were in black and white.

Q: What kind of jam can you not eat?
A: A traffic jam.

Fact: In 2010, a traffic jam on a highway in China went on for over a week and stretched 60 miles. People slept in their cars and were sold food by local vendors.

Q: Why couldn't the pirates play cards?
A: They were sitting on the deck!

Fact: Pirates wore earrings because they thought that they improved their eyesight - not as fashion accessories.

Q: What do you call a fake noodle?
A: An impasta.

Fact: Americans eat about 20 pounds of pasta a year but Italian eat way more at 60 pounds.

Q: What is a tornado's favorite game?
A: Twister!

Fact: Damage paths of tornadoes can be over one mile wide and 50 miles long.

Q: Where do Eskimos train their dogs?
A: In the mush-room!

Fact: Igloos are made of snow and ice but because these insulate well, igloos can be warm and comfortable inside.

Q: Why did the snowman call his dog Frost?
A: Because frost bites!

Fact: If you get frostbite don't rub the affected area. This could cause more tissue damage.

Q: What is the most religious insect?
A: A mosque-ito!

Fact: Mosquitoes are the deadliest insect on earth. More deaths are caused by illnesses mosquitoes spread than any other insect.

Q: What do you get if you cross the Lone Ranger with an insect?
A: The Masked-quito!

Fact: Only the female mosquito bites humans and animals.

Q: What's the biggest moth in the world?
A: A mammoth!

Fact: Woolly mammoths are extinct relatives of today's elephants. They lived during the last ice age, and they may have died off when the weather became warmer and their food supply changed.

Q: What are crisp, like milk and go 'eek, eek, eek' when you eat them?
A: Mice Krispies!

Fact: A mouse eats 15 - 20 times a day. Therefore they usually build their homes close to food sources.

Q: What is small, furry and brilliant at sword fights?
A: A mouseketeer!

Fact: Mice use their whiskers to sense changes in temperature and to help feel the surface they are walking along.

Q: What do you call an ant in space?
A: Cosmonants & Astronants!

Fact: Russia calls its astronauts cosmonauts, and the United States calls its astronauts.

Q: What medicine would you give an ill ant?
A: Antibiotics!

Fact: Antibiotics are medicines that work by treating or preventing bacterial infections.

Q: What is the biggest ant in the world?

A: An eleph-ant!

Fact: African elephants are actually fearful of guardian ants because they do not like them climbing up in their trunk and biting them.

Q: What do you get if you cross a grizzly bear and a harp?

A: A bear faced lyre!

Fact: Grizzly bears can weigh from 300 to 1,500 pounds and stand as tall as eight feet. Even though grizzly bears are extremely large they can run up to 35 miles per hour.

Q: What do you get if you cross a skunk with a bear?
A: Winnie the Pooh!

Fact: The best way to get rid of a skunk smell if sprayed is to apply a mixture of baking soda and hydrogen peroxide to the skin (with parental approval!)

Q: Why do bees hum?
A: Because they've forgotten the words!

Fact: The hum or buzz of bees is caused by their beating wings. Bees can beat their wings 230 times a second!

Q: How does a lion greet the other animals in the field?
A: 'Pleased to eat you.'!

Fact: The roar of a lion can be heard 5 miles away.

Q: What do you get if you cross a cat with a canary?
A: A peeping tom!

Fact: Coal miners used to bring singing canaries down into coal mines with them. If the canary stopped singing they knew they were running out of oxygen and needed to get out fast.

Q: What is a French cat's favorite pudding?
A: Chocolate mousse

Fact: Chocolate mousse is a whipped cream like dessert made from eggs, chocolate, and heavy cream. It's light and delicious!

Q: What happens when a hen eats gunpowder?
A: She lays hand gren-eggs!

Fact: Hand grenades are small explosive devices used in war that are often thrown toward the enemy where they explode.

Q: Why did the poor dog chase his own tail?
A: He was trying to make both ends meet!

Fact: Some dogs are able to use their tails to help them swim in water. Labrador retrievers especially use their tail in water.

Q: What do you get if you cross a cow with a camel?
A: Lumpy milkshakes!

Fact: Camels can drink 30 gallons of water in just 13 minutes!

Q: Why were the elephants thrown out of the swimming pool?
A: Because they couldn't hold their trunks up!

Fact: Young elephants especially enjoy swimming and diving in the water.

Q: Which fish can perform operations?
A: A Sturgeon!

Fact: Sturgeon are fish that live in lakes and rivers and some scientists say they have been around over 130 million years. They are called "living fossils" they have been around so long.

Q: What did the slug say as he slipped down the wall?
A: How slime flies!

Fact: A slug is a snail without a shell.

Q: Which fish go to heaven when they die?
A: Angelfish!

Fact: Don't let the name fool you, angel fish are no angels! They like to eat other creatures such as shrimp, insects, and bloodworms.

Q: What kind of horse can swim underwater without coming up for air?
A: A seahorse!

Fact: Seahorses prefer to swim in pairs with their tails linked together.

Q: What did one firefly say to the other?
A: Got to glow now!

Fact: Male fireflies that glow use their flash to attract females. Some fireflies synchronize their flashes.

Q: Why are spiders good swimmers?
A: They have webbed feet.

Fact: The diving bell spider can swim and spend most of its like below water. These spiders spin a web cocoon of silk which they then fill up with air creating a bubble that they can take with them underwater

Q: Why were the early days of history called the dark ages?
A: Because there were so many knights!

Fact: Being a knight in medieval times was extremely expensive. The armor, the weapons, the horse, and the servants all cost a lot of money.

Q: If there are ten cats in a boat and one jumps out, how many are left?
A: None, they were all copycats!

Fact: Cats sleep 70% of their lives.

Q: Teacher: Why does the Statue of Liberty stand in New York harbor?
A: Pupil: Because it can't sit down!

Fact: The Statue of Liberty was assembled on its pedestal after being constructed in France and sent to the USA in crates.

Q: Teacher: Why is the Mississippi such an unusual river?
A: Pupil: Because it has four eyes and can't see!

Fact: The length of the Mississippi River is approximately 2,320 miles. But the Missouri River is actually longer.

Q: Why did the teacher wear sunglasses?
A: Because his class was so bright!

Fact: The Chinese of the 12th Century are credited with inventing the first sunglasses, both to protect their eyes from the glare of the sun and to hide their facial expressions in a court of law.

Q: What did the bee say to the flower?
A: Hello honey!

Fact: Honey stored in air tight containers never spoils. Sealed honey vats found in King Tut's tomb still contained edible honey, despite over 2,000 years beneath the desert sands.

Q: When a knight in armor was killed in battle, what sign did they put on his grave?
A: Rust in peace!

Fact: A knight's armor was very heavy. It could weigh as much as 100 pounds!

Q: Teacher: What can you tell me about the Dead Sea?
A: Pupil: Dead? I didn't even know he was sick!

Fact: The Dead Sea, next to Israel, is not really a sea. It's a lake and has a lot of salt in it. All the salt can help a person easily float in it.

Q: Why is Alabama the smartest state in the USA?
A: Because it has 4 A's and one B!

Fact: In 1836, Alabama was the first state in the union to declare Christmas a legal holiday.

Q: What are prehistoric monsters called when they sleep?
A: A dinosnore!

Fact: Scientists believe we no longer have dinosaurs today because they went extinct due to an asteroid impact with the earth or because of volcano activity.

Q: Why do birds fly south in the winter?
A: Because it's too far to walk!

Fact: Actually, birds fly south in the winter to warmer climates where they can find more food.

Q: Did you hear about the mad scientist who put dynamite in his fridge?
A: They say it blew his cool!

Fact: Dynamite was invented by Alfred Nobel, the same guy who later established the Nobel Peace prize.

Q: How was the Roman Empire cut in half?
A: With a pair of Caesars!

Fact: Scissors were originally invented by the Egyptians in 1500 BC and then later improved by the Romans in 100 AD.

Q: Why did the lazy man want a job in a bakery?
A: So he could loaf around!

Fact: In 1943, the US government decided to ban sliced bread. It was an unpopular decision and quickly changed back.

Q: Why was the Egyptian girl confused?
A: Because her daddy was a mummy!

Fact: Egyptians mummified bodies to prepare them for life after death.

Q: Why is Russia a very fast country?
A: Because the people are always Russian!

Fact: Russia is the largest country in land in the world.

Q: Why did Mickey Mouse take a trip into space?
A: He wanted to find Pluto!

Fact: Pluto is so far away from the Sun that since its discovery in 1930, 85 years ago, it has not made one complete orbit of the Sun! It actually takes 247 earth years for Pluto to orbit the Sun.

Q: What is a cheerleader's favorite color?
A: Yeller!

Fact: Cheerleading was originally an all-male activity.

Q: Why are astronauts successful people?
A: Because they always go up in the world!

Fact: The United States has close to 300 million people living in it, but only 12 of these people have ever walked on the moon.

Q: Why did the cowboy die with his boots on?
A: Because he didn't want to stub his toe when he kicked the bucket!

Fact: Before trains and barbed wires fences the main work of cowboys was to tend cattle on long cattle drives to market.

Coming home from his Little League game, Billy swung open the front door very excited. Unable to attend the game, his father immediately wanted to know what happened. "So, how did you do son?" he asked.

"You'll never believe it!" Billy said. "I was responsible for the winning run!"

"Really? How'd you do that?"

"I dropped the ball."

Fact: The longest professional baseball game recorded was in 1984 and lasted 8 hours 6 minutes.

Q: How many letters are in The Alphabet?
A: There are 11 letters in The Alphabet.

Fact: The least commonly used letter in the English language is Z.

Q: What is a ghost's favorite position in soccer?
A: Ghoul keeper.

Fact: A professional soccer player runs about 4 miles in each game.

Q: What is a Cheerleader's favorite food?
A: Cheerios!

Fact: The Dallas Cowboys were the first NFL team to have recognized cheerleaders.

Q: Why did the basketball player go to jail?
A: Because he shot the ball.

Fact: The first basketball hoops were actually just peach baskets and the first backboards were made of wire.

Q: Why do basketball players love donuts?
A: Because they dunk them!

Fact: More injuries occur from playing basketball than from football.

Q: Why did the golfer wear two pairs of pants?
A: In case he got a hole in one!

Fact: Golf is one of only two sports played on the moon. Javelin throwing is the other.

Q: How is a baseball team similar to a pancake?
A: They both need a good batter!

Fact: The earliest known pancakes were made about 12,000 years ago from ground grains and nuts, mixed with water or milk and cooked on hot stones.

Q: What's a golfer's favorite letter?
A: Tee!

Fact: The chances of making two holes-in-one in a round of golf are one in 67 million.

Q: What animal is best at hitting a baseball?
A: A bat!

Fact: Bats can live more than 30 years and can fly at speeds of up to 60 miles per hour.

Q: At what sport to waiters do really well?
A: Tennis, because they can serve so well.

Fact: The fastest serve in tennis was by Samuel Groth who served the ball 163.4 miles per hour.

Q: How do baseball players stay cool?
A: They sit next to the fans.

Fact: Former professional baseball player Derek Jeter made $269,841.27 per at bat near the end of his career.

Q: Why is tennis such a loud sport?
A: The players raise a racquet.

Fact: There are five types of court surface used in professional play: Clay, Hard, Glass, Carpet and Wood.

Q: Why did the ballerina quit?
A: Because it was tu-tu hard!

Fact: One ballerina tutu (short skirt) costs up to $2,000 to make and requires 60-90 hours of labor and over 100 yards of ruffle.

Q: What is an insect's favorite sport?
A: Cricket!

Fact: Only male crickets chirp and do so to attract a female mate. They do so by rubbing their back legs together.

Q: What do hockey players and magicians have in common?
A: Both do hat tricks!

Fact: The fastest slap shot on record is Bobby Hull's, which was 118 miles per hour.

Q: Why did the man keep doing the backstroke?
A: Because he just ate and didn't want to swim on a full stomach!

Fact: Swimming strengthens the heart and lungs and works out all the major muscle groups.

Q: What is the hardest part about skydiving?
A: The ground!

Fact: The highest skydive was almost 25 miles high. The skydiver traveled so fast downward that he broke the sound barrier.

Q: Why did the book join the police?
A: He wanted to go undercover!

Fact: There are more than 900,000 sworn law enforcement officers now serving in the United States, which is the highest figure ever.

Q: Why was there thunder and lightning in the lab?
A: The scientists were brainstorming!

Fact: Thunder is caused by lightening. At any moment around 18,000 thunderstorms are taking place somewhere on Earth.

Q: What did the spider do on the computer?
A: Made a website!

Fact: There are over 1 billion websites on the World Wide Web.

Q: What did the computer do at lunchtime?
A: Had a byte!

Fact: A "bit" is the smallest piece of computer information. A "byte" is a combination of eight "bits."

Q: What does a baby computer call his father?
A: Data!

Fact: Computer data is information processed and stored on a computer. For example, a photograph on your computer would be computer data.

Q: Why did the computer keep sneezing?
A: It had a virus!

Fact: A computer virus is a program or piece of code downloaded to your computer that runs against your wishes. They are often attached to email.

Q: Why did the computer squeak?
A: Because someone stepped on its mouse!

Fact: Early versions of the computer mouse were called the computer turtle.

Q: Why was there a bug in the computer?
A: Because it was looking for a byte to eat?

Fact: A computer bug is an error or flaw in the computer that makes it not work like you want it to.

Q: What did one elevator say to the other elevator?
A: I think I'm coming down with something!

Fact: Elevators are safer than escalators and cars which have more accidents.

Q: Why can't your nose be 12 inches long?
A: Because then it would be a foot!

Fact: Your nose adds moisture to the air you breathe so your lungs won't dry out. It also cleans the air you breathe.

Q. What do you do with a dead chemist?

A: Barium (bury him).

Fact: Barium is a chemical element used for different things including in fireworks to give them their green color.

Q: Where do bees go on holiday?
A: Stingapore!

Fact: Honey bees never sleep, and they communicate with each other by dancing and by using pheromones.

Q. Why do chemists prefer nitrates?
A: Because they're cheaper than day rates.

Fact: Nitrates are salts that are often added to processed food to keep it fresh.

Q. Why is electricity so dangerous?
A: It doesn't conduct itself.

Fact: Electricity can be made from wind, water, the sun and even animal poop.

Q: Why did the ice cream cone take karate lessons?
A: It was tired of getting licked.

Fact: The ice cream cone was invented at the 1904 World's Fair in St. Louis, Missouri when the ice cream vendors ran out of bowls to serve ice cream in.

Q: Why can't you tell a joke while you're standing on ice?
A: Because it might crack up.

Fact: Three quarters of the fresh water in the entire world is contained in ice glaciers.

Q: What are the strongest creatures in the ocean?
A: Mussels.

Fact: Mussels are shellfish that filter water to find plankton (tiny microscopic organisms) to eat. Mussels are also eaten by humans and are high in protein.

As two caterpillars were crawling along, a butterfly flew overhead. One turned to the other and said, "You'll never get me up in one of those things!"

Fact: Caterpillars love to eat so they can get big and become a moth or butterfly. Usually the first meal of a caterpillar is its egg shell.

Q: What do firemen put in their soup?
A: Fire-crackers!

Fact: Firecrackers were invented 2000 years ago by the Chinese.

Q: What did the duck say when he bought lipstick?
A: Put it on my bill.

Fact: The average woman spends $15,000 on makeup in her lifetime — and of that amount, $1,780 goes toward lipstick.

Q: Why did the boy bring a ladder to school?
A: He thought it was a high school!

Fact: Never use an aluminum ladder when working around electricity. You could be shocked because metal allows electricity to travel very well.

An FBI agent is interviewing a bank teller after the bank had been robbed 3 times by the same bandit. "Did you notice anything special about the man?" asks the agent. "Yes," replies the teller. "He was better dressed each time."

Fact: Most robberies occur on the street, directly against a person, and are called a strong-arm robbery.

A sloth is out for a walk when he's mugged by four snails. After recovering his wits, he goes to make a police report. "Can you describe the snails?" asks the officer. "Not well, it all happened so fast," replies the sloth.

Fact: It takes up to a month for a sloth to digest one meal because of the tough leaves they feed on.

91

Q: If April showers bring May flowers then what do May flowers bring?
A: Pilgrims!

Fact: The Mayflower didn't land in Plymouth first. It first landed in Cape Cod.

Q: What's in the middle of a jellyfish?
A: A jellybutton

Fact: Jelly fish don't have brains. Instead that have nets of nerves that help them function.

Q: How do porcupines play leapfrog?
A: Very carefully

Fact: Baby porcupines have soft quills which quickly harden hours after they are born.

Q: Why do golfers take an extra pair of socks?

A: In case they get a hole in one.

Fact: Feet are one of the sweatiest parts of the body, and socks help to absorb the sweat.

Q: Why are giraffes so slow to apologize?

A: It takes them a long time to swallow their pride.

Fact: Giraffes spend most of their lives standing up; they even sleep standing up.

Q: What is a porcupine's favorite food?

A: Prickled onions.

Fact: Some porcupines are excellent swimmers. They like to eat tree bark, grass, twigs, stems, berries, and similar things.

Customer: How much is that duck?
Shopkeeper: Ten dollars.
Customer: Okay, could you please send me the bill?
Shopkeeper: I'm sorry, but you'll have to take the whole bird.

Fact: A duck waddles instead of walks because of its webbed feet.

Q: What season is it when you go on a trampoline?
A: Springtime.

Fact: The first trampoline was built in 1930s by George Nissen, a gymnast at the University of Iowa, who got the idea from examining circus nets

Q: What kind of bow can't be tied?
A: A rainbow.

Fact: No two people see the same rainbow, in fact even our individual eyes see slightly different rainbows.

Q: What do you call a bear with no teeth?
A: A gummy bear!

Fact: The name "gummy" in gummy bears comes from the main ingredient called "gum arabic," which is resin from the Acacia tree.

Q: Why did the moon feel sick to its stomach?
A: It was a full moon.

Fact: It takes 27.3 days for the moon to circle the earth. It takes the Earth 365 days to circle the Sun.

Q: What did the skunks do on Saturday night?
A: They watched a movie on their smell-evision.

Fact: Skunks have excellent hearing and an excellent sense of smell; however, they have poor vision.

Q: Why couldn't the skeletons play any music?
A: They don't have any organs.

Fact: Our muscles, organs, and skin hand on our skeleton. Without a skeleton we couldn't survive.

Q: What did the almond say to the psychiatrist?
A: "Everybody says I'm nuts!"

Fact: Almonds are good for you and great at fighting diseases.

Q: What did the tornado say to the race car?
A: "Can I take you for a spin?"

Fact: The USA averages around 1200 tornadoes every year, more than any other country.

Q: What happened to the dog after it swallowed a watch?
A: It was full of ticks.

Fact: Ticks are arachnids. Meaning, they are more closely related to spiders and scorpions than insects.

Q: Why did the meteorite go to Hollywood?
A: It wanted to be a star.

Fact: Millions of meteorites travel through Earth's atmosphere each day. When a meteor encounters our atmosphere it is vaporized in a ball of fire.

Q: What do you get when you throw noodles in a Jacuzzi?
A: Spa-ghetti.

Fact: Jacuzzis are big tubs with hot water jets people enjoy soaking in. The name Jacuzzi comes from the last name of seven brothers who invented the Jacuzzi.

Q: What kind of bugs like to sneak up on you?
A: Spy-ders.

Fact: Spiders have 8 legs while insects have 6. Spiders don't have antennae like insects do.

Q: Why do bees have sticky hair?
A: Because of the honey combs!

Fact: Two tablespoons of honey would fuel a honey bee flying once around the world.

Q: Why did the pig have to sit on the bench during football practice?
A: He pulled his ham-string.

Fact: Your hamstring muscles run from your behind bones to the back of your knees. You pull a hamstring when you tear some of the muscles in that area.

Q: Why couldn't all the king's horses and all the king's men put Humpty Dumpty together again?
A: They were egghausted.

Fact: Most people think that Humpty Dumpty in the children's nursery rhyme refers to an egg. Actually, Humpty Dumpty was the nickname given to a canon used in the English Civil War. The canon fell from the walls and none of the king's horses or men were able to recover it.

Q: What do garbage collectors eat for lunch?
A: Junk food!

Fact: Glass never wears out and can be recycled over and over.

Q: Why are possums so lazy?
A: All they do is hang around.

Fact: Possums can hang from their tails for a short period of time, but they don't sleep hanging from their tails as some people think.

Q: What do you call four bullfighters in quicksand?
A: Cuatro sinko.

Fact: Slow movements in quicksand to free yourself are more effective than quick movements with a lot of struggling.

Q: Who keeps the ocean clean?
A: The mer-maid.

Fact: Scientists say that in the Pacific Ocean, between the United States and Japan, there is a large patch of garbage that is swirling in the water just below the surface. It's mostly made up of plastic trash.

Q: Why did the invisible man turn down a job offer?
A: He just couldn't see himself doing it.

Fact: Scientists are getting closer to inventing an invisibility cloak. It works by bending light so you can't see the person behind the cloak.

Q: What happens when race car drivers eat too much?
A: They get Indy-gestion.

Fact: The Indianapolis Motor Speedway is the world's largest spectator sporting facility, with more than 250,000 permanent seats.

Q: What kind of tree has the best bark?
A: A dogwood.

Fact: Aspirin, one of the most used medicines in the world, comes from the bark of the Willow tree.

Q: Why wouldn't the lion eat the clown?
A: He tasted funny.

Fact: Lions spend between 16 and 20 hours each day resting and sleeping. They have few sweat glands so they wisely tend to conserve their energy by resting during the day and become more active at night when it is cooler.

Q: What should you do when you get in a jam?
A: Grab some bread and peanut butter.

Fact: The average child will eat 1,500 peanut butter and jelly sandwiches before graduating from high school.

Q: How can you go surfing in the kitchen?

A: On a micro-wave.

Fact: Hawaiians referred to surfing as *he'enalu*, which means "wave sliding."

Q: What is the difference between boogers and broccoli?

A: Kids won't eat their broccoli.

Fact: Broccoli is very high in Vitamin A. Vitamin A helps to fight cancer in your cells and helps keep your eyes healthy.

Q: How did Thomas Edison invent the lightbulb?

A: He got a bright idea.

Fact: We say "Hello" today when we answer the telephone because Thomas Edison was the first to do this.

Q: What kind of button won't you find at a sewing store?
A: A belly button.

Fact: Only mammals, such as yourself, have belly buttons. Non-mammals, such as birds that are laid in an egg don't have belly buttons.

Q: Did you hear about the actor who fell through the floor?
A: It was just a stage he was going through!

Fact: Actors and actresses are also called Thespians.

Q: Why did the hamburger always lose the race?
A: It could never ketchup.

Fact: Early ketchup was not made from tomatoes. It was made from anchovies, shallots, oysters, lemons, or walnuts.

Q: What was the best time of day in the Middle Ages?
A: Knight-time.

Fact: Young knights would first learn to fight on the back of pigs. They would learn balance and skills for mounted combat.

Q: Why did the skunk have to stay in bed until it felt better?
A: It was the doctor's odors.

Fact: Skunks often attack beehives because they eat honeybees.

Q: Why did the sparrow go to the library?
A: It was looking for some bookworms.

Fact: The male sparrow is responsible for building of the nest. During construction, the male will try to attract a female.

Q: What is a bat's motto?
A: Hang in there.

Fact: Bats can find their food in total darkness. They locate insects by emitting inaudible high-pitched sounds, 10-20 beeps per second and listening to echoes.

Q: How do you shoot a bumble bee?
A: With a bee-bee gun.

Fact: Only female bumble bees sting. Male bumble bees don't have a stinger at all.

Q: What do you call a lazy kangaroo?
A: A pouch potato.

Fact: Kangaroos are the only large animal to use hopping as their primary method of moving. Hopping is a fast and energy efficient means of travelling which allows them to cover large distances in places where there is little food and water available.

PART TWO

RIDDLES

Q: I'm tall when I'm young and I'm short when I'm old. What am I?
A: A candle

Fact: For thousands of years, up to the 1900s, candles were the main source of light in darkness.

Q: Poor people have it. Rich people need it. If you eat it you die. What is it?
A: Nothing

Fact: Roughly 74 percent of the universe is "nothing," or what physicists call dark energy.

Q: If I drink, I die. If I eat, I am fine. What am I?
A: A fire!

Fact: Flames are the part of a fire which we can see, they can be different colors, depending on the substance which is burning.

**Q: In a one-story pink house, there was a pink person, a pink cat, a pink fish, a pink computer, a pink chair, a pink table, a pink telephone, a pink shower– everything was pink!
What color were the stairs?**
A: There weren't any stairs, it was a one story house!

Fact: The color pink is named after the flowering plant called Pinks. Pink is a combination of the colors red and white.

Q: What goes up when rain comes down?
A: An umbrella!

Fact: Rain occurs on other planets in our Solar System but it is different than the rain we experience here on Earth. For example, rain on Venus is made of sulfuric acid and due to the intense heat it evaporates before it even reaches the surface!

Q: A dad and his son were riding their bikes and crashed. Two ambulances came and took them to different hospitals. The man's son was in the operating room and the doctor said, "I can't operate on you. You're my son."
How is that possible?
A: The doctor is his mom!

Fact: To become a doctor, you will need to study biology, chemistry, physics, math, and English. It is not easy to get into medical school. You have to do very well in college and on medical school entrance tests.

Q: What has 4 eyes but can't see?
A: Mississippi

Fact: Barq's Root Beer was invented in Biloxi, Mississippi in 1898 by Edward Adolf Barq, Sr.

Q: If I have it, I don't share it. If I share it, I don't have it. What is it?
A: A Secret.

Fact: One secret of Disney World is that "smellitzers" are placed in different locations to spray scents that smell like baked cookies and vanilla.

Q: What has hands but cannot clap?
A: A clock

Fact: Quartz is used in some clocks to keep time. This is because quartz pulsates in one second intervals.

Q: What can you catch but not throw?
A: A cold.

Fact: Most grown-ups have two to four colds a year; children can easily get six to 10.

Q: Two girls were born on the same day, same year, same parents, except they are not twins. Explain:
A: They are triplets.

Fact: Most triplets do not look exactly alike.

Q: A house has 4 walls. All of the walls are facing south, and a bear is circling the house. What color is the bear?
A: The house is on the North Pole, so the bear is white.

Fact: There is no land at the North Pole. Only floating ice.

Q: If an electric train is travelling south, which way is the smoke going?
A: There is no smoke, it's an electric train!

Fact: Some trains can reach speeds over 186 miles per hour!

Q: What has one eye but cannot see?
A: A needle

Fact: Most needles today are made of steel. Early needles, however, were made of bone.

Q: A man leaves home and turns left three times, only to return home facing two men wearing masks. Who are those two men?
A: A Catcher and Umpire.

Fact: Baseball umpires are responsible for officiating the game, including beginning and ending the game, enforcing the rules of the game and the grounds, making judgment calls on plays, and handling the disciplinary actions.

Q: Which weighs more, a pound of feathers or a pound of bricks?
A: Neither, they both weigh one pound!

Fact: Preening (straightening and cleaning feathers with the beak) keeps feathers moist and flexible, and maintains waterproofing.

Q: A frog jumped into a pot of cream and started treading. He soon felt something solid under his feet and was able to hop out of the pot. What did the frog feel under his feet?
A: The frog felt butter under his feet, because he churned the cream and made butter.

Fact: It takes 21 pints of milk to make one pound of butter.

Q: How many months have 28 days?
A: All 12 months!

Fact: Months are based roughly on the moon. A lunar month is 29 1/2 days, or the time from one new moon to the next.

Q: If a blue house is made out of blue bricks, a yellow house is made out of yellow bricks and a pink house is made out of pink bricks, what is a green house made of?
A: Glass.

Fact: A greenhouse is a building or part of a building that has glass walls and a glass roof and is used for growing plants.

Q: What has Eighty-eight keys but can't open a single door?
A: A piano.

Fact: There are 7500 working parts in the body of each piano.

Q: Mr. Blue lives in the blue house, Mr. Pink lives in the pink house, and Mr. Brown lives in the brown house. Who lives in the white house?
A: The President!

Fact: The White House requires 570 gallons of paint to cover its outside surface.

Q: They come out at night without being called, and are lost in the day without being stolen. What are they?
A: Stars.

Fact: Every star in the night sky is bigger and brighter than our own Sun if you were as close to it as you are to our Sun.

Q: Tuesday, Sam and Peter went to a restaurant to eat lunch. After eating lunch, they paid the bill. But Sam and Peter did not pay the bill, so who did?
A: Their friend, Tuesday.

Fact: Tuesday is the day that bosses say they get the most work done from their employees.

Q: A monkey, a squirrel, and a bird are racing to the top of a coconut tree. Who will get the banana first, the monkey, the squirrel, or the bird?
A: None of them, because you can't get a banana from a coconut tree!

Fact: The white, fleshy part of the coconut is called coconut meat.

Q: Three people were in a boat. They all fell off. Only two people ended up with wet hair. Why didn't the other person's hair get wet?
A: Because he was bald!

Fact: Wearing hats does not cause baldness.

Q: What can you hear but not touch or see?
A: Your voice.

Fact: The sound of each individual's voice is unique and depends on the shape and size of that persons' vocal cords and the size of the rest of their body.

Q: What loses its head in the morning but gets it back at night?
A: A pillow.

Fact: In Asia, it's common to fill pillows with buckwheat.

Q: Jack rode into town on Friday and rode out 2 days later on Friday. How can that be possible?
A: Friday is his horse's name!

Fact: Friday is considered by bosses to be the least productive day of the week for their employees.

Q: What has a head, a tail, is brown, and has no legs?
A: A penny!

Fact: Pennies were the very first coins minted in the United States, and pennies last about 25 years.

Q: What goes up, but never comes down?
A: Your age!

Fact: People say they are the happiest when they are young and when they are old. Middle age seems to be the least happy time.

Q: What starts with a P and ends with an E and has a million letters in it?
A: Post Office!

Fact: There is still one place in the United States where mail travels by mule. That is to a town down in the Grand Canyon.

Q. It's been around for millions of years, but it's no more than a month old. What is it?
A: The moon.

Fact: If you were on the moon, you would weigh much less than you weigh on earth.

Q. I went to London and have been to Rome. I could go to India and sometimes I get sent home. I do all of this by simply sitting in a corner. What am I?
A: A stamp.

Fact: The first stamps issued in the USA had no sticky substance on the back. The stamps had to be pinned or sewed to the letter.

Q. I can be long or I can be short. I can be grown and I can be bought. I can be painted or left bare. I can be round or even square. What am I?
A: Fingernails.

Fact: After you are sick, your nails grow faster than normal. Also, males' nails grow faster than females' nails, except when she is pregnant.

Q: I have no eyes and no legs. I have no ears and am strong enough to move the earth. What am I?
A: A worm.

Fact: Earthworms do not have lungs and breathe air through their skin.

Q. What has to be broken before you can use it?
A: An egg.

Fact: White chickens tend to lay white eggs, and brown chickens tend to lay brown eggs. The color of the egg makes no difference in nutrition.

Made in the USA
Columbia, SC
24 October 2021

47717266R00074